WE ARE
Palestinian

A CELEBRATION OF CULTURE AND TRADITION

Crocodile Books, USA

An imprint of Interlink Publishing Group, Inc.

www.interlinkbooks.com

For Seedo Mustafa, whose stories,
and love, I was lucky to have grown up with.
- R.K.

First published in 2023 by

Crocodile Books
An imprint of Interlink Publishing Group, Inc.
46 Crosby Street
Northampton, Massachusetts 01060
www.interlinkbooks.com

Text copyright © Reem Kassis 2023
Illustrated by Noha Eilouti

Published simultaneously in the UK by Studio Press,
an imprint of Bonnier Books UK

American edition publisher: Michel Moushabeck
Edited by Saaleh Patel and Frankie Jones
Designed by Rob Ward
Production by Emma Kidd

Library of Congress Cataloging-in-Publication Data:
LCCN Permalink: https://lccn.loc.gov/2023012340
ISBN 978-1-62371-725-4

Printed and bound in Malaysia

3 5 7 9 10 8 6 4 2

WE ARE
Palestinian

A CELEBRATION OF CULTURE AND TRADITION

WRITTEN BY REEM KASSIS & ILLUSTRATED BY NOHA EILOUTI

Contents

We Are Palestinian

There is an area, the shape of a crescent moon, stretching from Egypt up the eastern coast of the Mediterranean Sea and across to the Persian Gulf, often called the Fertile Crescent. Its land is lush and bountiful. It is also called the Cradle of Civilization because it's a place where culture and many innovations—including writing, the wheel, agriculture and the use of irrigation—were born. Do you know one of the countries located in that area? Yes, you guessed it, Palestine!

The native people who have inhabited this land for millennia are called Palestinians. During this time, empires rose and fell, languages changed, religions evolved and many powerful civilizations—Greeks, Romans, Persians, Arabs, Jews, Crusaders, Ottomans—passed through and left a mark on this place and its people. Because of this, the culture of Palestinians in Palestine is vast and rich.

From the foods we eat, like *maqlubeh* (p 70) and *ka'ak al quds* (p 76), to the *zajal* (p 86) music we sing and the *dabke* (p 84) we dance, there is so much that makes Palestinian life so special. But Palestine is also closely connected to its neighbors—Syria, Lebanon, Jordan, Egypt—and at various points in history we were like one land. There was so much travel and trade happening between our people that you see many commonalities across our region too: like the hummus and falafel (p 78) that everybody eats, the native plants (p 66) we forage for and the religions we practice.

One of the main things that contributes to the rich culture of Palestine is its people. Our writers, poets, creative thinkers, performing artists and painters hold their homeland close to their hearts. Their contributions keep our shared history and traditions alive from one generation to the next.

When I started to write this book, I imagined my daughters, two strong Palestinian girls, growing up away from their homeland. I wanted them to know how beautiful their culture is and that they can take part in and be proud of it no matter where they are in the world. But then I started to worry! Even a book of a thousand pages would not be enough to encompass all the traditions, cultural symbols and creative people that make Palestinian culture and history as beautiful as they are.

So, with my daughters and you, young reader, in mind, I chose some of the people and topics that I thought could excite, engage, inform and inspire. I hope this quick introduction to Palestinian culture gives you a glimpse into its vastness and greatness so that you are encouraged to explore it more.

Geography

There are so many beautiful places in Palestine that it would be impossible to cover them all. So in this section, we're going to explore some of the most famous cities and find out what makes them so special. Some of these cities are now in Israel, but they still have big Palestinian populations, and our culture and rich history flourishes in the landmarks and traditions.

Jerusalem

Jerusalem is one of the oldest cities on Earth; traces of civilization there go back 6000 years. In that time, it has been destroyed, captured and recaptured—but it has survived, and remains a very special place. One reason is that it is the holy city for the three major Abrahamic religions: Judaism, Christianity and Islam. The major landmarks for these religions—the Western Wall, the Church of the Holy Sepulchre, the Garden Tomb and the Dome of the Rock and Al-Aqsa Mosque—are all in Jerusalem.

Although Jerusalem is a big city today, its core is the Old City of Jerusalem, which is surrounded by a giant wall that was built around 500 years ago during the Ottoman Empire.

Fun Fact

The wall surrounding the Old City is about 2.5 miles / 4000 meters long—that's about 12 Eiffel Towers lying on their side!

The wall has 34 watchtowers and seven gates made of beautiful Jerusalem stone—strong, cream-colored limestone or dolomite rock. Inside, the city has been divided in different ways over the years, but today it has four quarters: Muslim, Christian, Armenian and Jewish.

The streets are made of massive stone slabs and cars cannot drive inside the city walls. When you walk its streets, you see beautiful artisan craft and antique stores lining the sides, owned by the same families for generations. You can smell fragrant spices and buy delicious food, from *ka'ak al quds* to falafel and *knafeh*. Outside the city walls, Jerusalem is now divided into East and West Jerusalem. The Western side is where most of the Jewish Israelis live, and the Eastern side is where the Palestinians live.

Gaza

Gaza is a Palestinian territory that borders Egypt on one side and Israel on the other. It is made up of five main areas, the largest of which is Gaza City. It is also one of the most densely populated places on Earth. This means that there are many people living in a very small space.

Most of the people in Gaza are refugees—people who fled their homes because of war. They came from other places in Palestine, like Yaffa and Ramla and even far north like the Galilee. They hoped they would be able to go back after the 1948 Arab–Israeli War, but have now been displaced for over 75 years.

Gaza was once famous for its beautiful beaches on the Mediterranean Sea and its fishing industry. Now Israel's control of the waters restricts Gazan fishermen from going far out to sea to fish, which means it's increasingly difficult to make a living as a fisherman. Unfortunately, Gaza is also practically sealed off from the rest of the country, making it almost impossible for anyone to visit or leave it.

Did you know?

There are about two million people living in Gaza, a place the same size as the US city of Detroit, which has a population of 672,000.

While these things are sad, the people of Gaza are strong and hopeful, and we can learn many lessons from them about how to live life in the face of hardship. Famous artists like Malak Mattar (p 50) who paints beautiful pictures, and musicians like Mohammed Assaf (p 88) are from Gaza. On a day-to-day basis, the people of Gaza do the same activities people across the world do, like going to school, working, cooking, even singing and dancing.

Supported and empowered by their families, their faith and by each other, the people of Gaza continue to live their lives.

Jericho

People believe that Jericho is the oldest city in the world. It is also the lowest city on Earth, sitting 258 meters below sea level. To understand what that means, picture yourself walking away from the beach and hiking down a valley—you would have to go down about 80 flights of stairs to reach Jericho.

The name of the valley it sits in is Wadi Qelt, which itself sits in the larger Jordan Valley in the West Bank.

People have always lived in Jericho, from the age of hunter gatherers to the present day. It's also one of the first places in the world to have agriculture and probably where irrigation, the process of supplying water to plants, was invented. It is the kind of city you call an oasis, or a fertile land in a desert environment. Ein es-Sultan (or The Sultan's Spring), which produces about 1000 gallons of water per minute, is what waters the whole area.

Did you know?

When archaeologists explored Jericho, they found remains of early settlements going back 11,000 years!

Jericho can get hot in the summer, but its winters are quite mild, rarely dipping below 50°F (10°C). This pleasant weather makes it a very popular place to visit for both Palestinians and tourists. People from all over the world visit Jericho to see its rich history, and visit landmarks like Hisham's Palace, an ancient castle built over 1200 years ago during the Ummayad Dynasty.

Fun Fact

More than 40,000 people visit Hisham's Palace each year.

Akka & Haifa

Akka and Haifa are two cities in the Galilee region with very rich histories that go back thousands of years. In that time, these cities have been conquered and ruled by many people. Today they are both under Israeli rule, but their populations are mixed between Palestinians and Jews.

Akka has always been an important city because of its location on a route between Syria and Egypt. It's so important, in fact, that even Napoleon Bonaparte tried to take it over. But Akka's people were so strong that he was not able to and he eventually retreated.

There is so much history and so many important landmarks in Akka that the whole city is a UNESCO world heritage site. The Wall of Akka is one of the most recognizable sights, especially the southern part that shields the city from the Mediterranean sea.

Of course, if you get hungry, you can have some of the best hummus in the country, hand-pounded by the same families that have been doing so for generations.

Haifa is a city built on the slopes of a mountain called Jabal al Karmil. Its most famous landmark is the Baha'í Gardens, a set of 19 terraces and over 1500 steps going up the mountain to a shrine that is holy in the Baha'í religion. This religion is relatively new, founded only about 150 years ago. Its main teaching is that all religions and people are worthy, and it is important for people to come together and be good to one another.

Haifa is a hub—a center—for Palestinian culture. It has many Palestinian-owned theaters, cafes, restaurants and nightclubs that host cultural discussions, art exhibitions, and many more fun events.

Yaffa & Nazareth

Yaffa was built on a hill, with a very wide view of the Mediterranean Sea coastline, making it an important city throughout history for trade. The 1936–1939 Arab revolt started there, and it was the site of many battles during the 1948 Arab–Israeli War. There were about 80,000 Palestinians in Yaffa before the war started, but by the end only around 4000 remained—the rest had been forced to leave, becoming refugees.

Today it has a mixed population of Jews and Palestinians.

The Clock Tower and the Yaffa Lighthouse are two of the most recognizable landmarks in Yaffa. Even if you have never been to Yaffa, you have probably eaten something from there—the Jaffa oranges. Those who are lucky to live in this beautiful city eat delicious seafood, citrus fruit and fresh bread from its many famous bakeries.

The city of Nazareth has no shortage of delicious bakeries selling sweets like baklava and burma either. But it is famous for much bigger things! It is the largest city in the northern part of the country and although in Israel, it has a predominantly Palestinian population.

Fun Fact

Aroos al Bahar, or Bride of the Sea, is what most Palestinians call Yaffa because of how beautiful it is.

Did you know?

Nazareth was the childhood home of Jesus! Kaneesat al Bishara (The Basilica of the Annunciation) is where the angel Gabriel is believed to have told the Virgin Mary that she was carrying a baby. That's why Jesus is often called "Jesus of Nazareth."

Although it is a very important city for Christians, it is home to a mixed population of faiths, with many Christian and Muslim citizens. There are many churches as well as mosques—the most famous and oldest being Al Masjid al Abyad (The White Mosque).

Regardless of religion, Nazareth has in recent years become an important place for many Palestinians living in Israel, who very proudly display their Palestinian culture.

Al Khalil (Hebron) & Nablus

Nablus and Al Khalil are the two largest cities in the West Bank area of Palestine.

Al-Khalil, or Hebron as it's known in the English-speaking world, is the largest. Like many other places in Palestine, Hebron is also a UNESCO world heritage site, a special place that needs to be safeguarded because it contains so much history. Its most famous and oldest landmark is Al-Haram al-Ibrahimi (Cave of the Patriarchs), a series of caves very holy to both Jews and Muslims. Today, the structure above the caves is split into a mosque and synagogue.

Nablus lies hidden in a valley between mountains that overlook the surrounding areas. This gave it a historically strategic position between two ancient routes, making it easy

Did you know?

Al-Khalil is also known for its handicrafts, like blown glass, and its food! It is the place to buy dibs, a molasses made from grapes, and malban—a yummy fruit leather made from grape juice filled with seeds. Al-Khalil is also famous for its jameed, a dried and fermented yogurt used to make mansaf, and of course for qidreh—a traditional dish of rice and meat cooked in special copper pots in communal town ovens.

Did you know?

One of the things Nablus was known for, and the largest item it traded, was soap. Sabon nabulsi, made from olive oil, was turned into a beautiful creamy-white block. To this day, there are many soap makers in Nablus, and you can see the soap stacked up into beautiful towers, ready to be purchased.

Whatever you do and wherever you study, though, everybody has to eat, and Nablus is famous across the world for its *knafeh* (p 74).

for Nablus to conduct trade across the Arab world.

Nablus is also an education and healthcare hub with six hospitals and the largest Palestinian university, An-Najah National University.

AL-JAMAL SOAP
Olive Oil Soap
Shower Soap

صابون الجمل المعزول

نابلس   منح

Bethlehem & Ramallah

Bethlehem and Ramallah are two Palestinian cities in the West Bank with fascinating histories.

Fun Fact

It is believed that Jesus was born in the city of Bethlehem.

Today, many tourists visit this city, especially around Christmas, to see the Church of the Nativity—the oldest continuously used place of worship in the Christian world.

Artisans from Bethlehem make beautiful items out of olive wood. No trip to Bethlehem is complete without purchasing a souvenir! The women of Bethlehem are also recognized for their very special tatreez (p 30) which combines gold and silver threads to make floral patterns and gorgeous traditional Palestinian bridal wear.

Ramallah is the city where the Palestinian Authority is located. It is famous for having a very lively cultural and culinary scene—there are many theaters and museums as well as countless restaurants and hotels.

In addition to The Palestinian Museum and the Yasser Arafat Museum, Ramallah also has a museum dedicated to the Palestinian poet Mahmoud Darwish (p 38). Surrounding Ramallah are many smaller yet still famous Palestinian towns, such as Birzeit—home to Birzeit University—and Taybeh, home to Taybeh beer and Al-Khadr church, which dates back to the Byzantine era. If you ever visit these two cities, you will have plenty to do, see and eat.

Fun Fact

One of the most famous places in Ramallah is Booza Rukab—an ice cream shop founded in the 1930s. Its delicious ice cream is made from a gum resin, giving it a stretchy texture and sweet taste.

Cultural Symbols

We all like to know that we belong: to a family, to a group or to a nation. This makes us feel comfortable and safe and loved. But countries are so big that we need specific things we can all recognize and easily share in to feel that sense of belonging. Some things are created specifically for that purpose—like the flag and the national anthem. Other things become national symbols simply because we have used them for so long or because they played an important role in our history—like tatreez (p 30) and the keffiya (p 35). Because many Palestinians live outside of Palestine now, we hold on to these cultural symbols very strongly because they help us feel like we have pieces of our home everywhere in the world.

National Anthem & Flag

A flag is probably the strongest symbol of a country. While all countries have flags, the design of each flag, and what its different colors and symbols mean, changes from country to country. For Palestinians, like many other Arab countries, our flag is made of four colors: red, black, green and white. It has three horizontal lines—black, white and green—with a red triangle based at the hoist (the edge nearest to the flagpole).

The other strong symbol of national identity is the national anthem: a song that all people from a country know represents their homeland. Usually, people can sing the anthem too, and recognize it as soon as they hear it.

Our national anthem for many years was a song called

Did you know?

Some people say most Arab flags are made of the same four colors because an old Arab poet once said, "our deeds are white, our realities are black, our pastures are green, and our past is red." The poet was probably referring to the idea that Arabs are good people, that they face a difficult reality and though they live in a fertile land, they have experienced a sad past.

national anthem and you can hear this song all over the radio, at school performances and even in concerts.

"Mawtini," which means "my homeland." It was written by the Palestinian poet Ibrahim Tuqan who was a member of the Tuqan family that governed the Palestinian city of Nablus during the 18th and 19th centuries. His sister, Fadwa Tuqan, also wrote many poems and their poems are still very popular today.

A couple of decades ago, the Palestinian government decided to change it to a song called "Fida'i," which means "warrior." While that song is beautiful too, almost all Palestinians still consider "Mawtini" to be the

Handala

Handala is a very special boy. He was born at 10 years old, and even now, about 50 years later, he is still a 10-year-old boy. Handala is upset. He has his head bent down and he is barefoot, with sparse, spiky hair and shabby clothes; like many refugees, he does not have access to much. What is most striking is that his hands are clasped behind

Did you know?

Handala is a caricature: a drawing or picture imitating a real person. Even though Handala is the most famous Palestinian caricature of all time, we don't really know what he looks like because he has his back turned to us.

his back. He shows us that he's in protest, and is standing up against what is happening to Palestinians.

Naji Al-Ali, the artist who dreamed up Handala, was 10 years old when he was forced to leave his home in Palestine. He sketched Handala many years later to represent how Palestinians felt about having to leave their homeland. Naji Al-Ali said that Handala will remain 10 years old, just like he was when he left, and that he will only start to grow up when he is able to return to Palestine.

Naji Al-Ali was not able to return to Palestine before he died. He spent many years forced to move from place to place—Lebanon, Kuwait, London—but he was never allowed back to his home. Handala, on the other hand, is still alive because Palestinians, and people all over the world, know him and know that, although he may be a small child, he is very tough. So he will stay standing, waiting for the day Palestinians can go back to Palestine, and then maybe he will turn around, show us his face, and smile.

Did you know?

Handala has become such an important symbol that the design is often seen on jewelry, clothing, stationery and much more and is a way for Palestinians to proudly display their culture.

Tatreez

> ## Fun Fact
>
> Tatreez is a Palestinian embroidery practice and is done by threading a needle through fabric to make pretty designs.

Embroidery has been around since the start of civilization and every culture has its own designs and methods. The embroidery from the Arab world, and Palestine in particular, is said to be one of the richest and most beautiful in the world. It's so special that UNESCO (an organization that tries to protect the cultural traditions of the world) put Palestinian embroidery on their list of traditions that we need to safeguard for the future.

Most of us will recognize Palestinian embroidery as the cross-stitch patterns we see on *thobes* (Palestinian traditional dresses, p 32) or on cushions and tablecloths and other decorative fabrics.

Did you know?

There are so many kinds of tatreez. In fact, every village in Palestine used to have its own version of tatreez. Every one of those designs told a story: about where the person was from, or what kind of animals and plants were in that village, or what legends and beliefs people had.

how continued to embroider— not just for themselves, but as a job to make some money. Thanks to these women, and many others who write about it in books and teach us how to do it, tatreez has survived and become a Palestinian national symbol; it reminds us of our home and our history. That is why even today, almost any Palestinian home you go into will have something with tatreez on it.

Women would learn how to stitch from a young age and they would embroider their own dresses, accessories and all the fabrics they used in their homes.

As life moved forward and became harder for Palestinians after the war (p 98), many of the old traditions were lost. People started wearing more simple clothes and many girls were not taught how to embroider. But the Palestinian women who knew

Thobe & Gold Hat

Today, people tend to dress very similarly to one another. Two people living on opposite sides of the world may well buy clothes made in the same factories. But many years ago, it was not like that—you could tell where a person was from based on the clothes they wore. Now we call these clothes "the national dress" because they tell us what country a person is from. Even if people don't wear these outfits every day any more, many still wear them for special occasions like weddings, holidays or national celebrations.

The Palestinian national outfit for women is beautiful and detailed. The designs vary from village to village and from countryside to city, but they all have the main elements in common.

The traditional dress for Palestinian women includes a headdress. This changes based on where you come from, but there is nearly always a scarf called

mandeel that flies down the sides of the body and is kept in place with a hat or headband. These hats and headbands highlight where a woman is from and her social class. Sometimes these headdresses are embroidered, other times they can be filled with so many gold coins it is almost too heavy to wear! Those are usually kept for weddings and the coins are considered part of the bride's dowry (wedding gift).

Hatta & Egal

Men in Palestine have a traditional dress too. The main elements of it are the *sirwal*: a loose pantaloon that is tighter at the ankles, and the *qumbaz*: a robe that is worn over the top then folded over and tied with a belt.

But the most important part of this outfit is the *hatta* and *egal*, which many Arab men wear a version of even today.

A *hatta* is a very large square scarf, usually white and made of cotton, folded into a triangle and then draped over a man's head. The *egal* is a circular black band—think of two ropes shaped into a circle—that keeps the *hatta* in place.

Fun Fact

Archaeologists have found images of people in the Arab world wearing a hatta and egal going back hundreds of years.

In Palestine, the most famous kind of *hatta* is a *keffiya*, which is the same white square scarf but with a black fishnet pattern sewn on it. It used to be that a *keffiya* signaled someone was from the countryside, while a

tarboosh, a red hat with a black tassel that looks like an upside-down mug, signaled someone was from the city. Today, however, a *keffiya* symbolizes that someone is Palestinian, or supports Palestinians, and people across the world wear it—men and women alike—sometimes draped over the head like a *hatta* and other times simply tied around the neck like a scarf.

Today, the *keffiya* is one of the most recognizable Palestinian symbols. Yasser Arafat, the first president of the Palestinian National Authority almost always wore one on his head, draped to the side in a not-so-traditional way, and helped increase its popularity across the world.

Creative Minds

There are hundreds, if not thousands, of Palestinian thinkers, writers and artists who have made our culture the rich one it is today. Even a giant encyclopedia would not do justice to all their beautiful work and ideas. The creative thinkers in this chapter are just a very small selection. Some, you may have heard of countless times. Others, you may not recognize, so this will be the first time you learn about their contribution. As a group, they show a diverse cross-section of creative Palestinians from poets and painters to children's authors, professors and cultural change-makers. Just remember, this is only the tip of the iceberg. There are many more wonderful people to discover.

Mahmoud Darwish

1941–2008

Mahmoud Darwish was born in al-Birwa in Palestine, a village that no longer exists. But as a poet, Mahmoud Darwish kept al-Birwa, and much of Palestine's history, alive with his words.

Did you know?

When Mahmoud was a little boy, he dreamed of becoming a poet. His mother was illiterate—she could not read or write—so his grandfather taught him how to read.

During the 1948 war, when Mahmoud was six years old, he and his family became refugees in Lebanon. They returned a year later to find their village and home were gone. Mahmoud was very sad, but he loved to write and writing gave him comfort, so he started to write poetry when he was seven years old. By the time he was 19, he published his first poetry book called *Asafir bila ajniha*, or *Birds without Wings*.

In his twenties, he lived in Haifa and worked as a journalist and editor. Sometimes his writing made people angry. This led to him being sent to prison many times and being banned from traveling. Finally, when he was 30, Mahmoud was able to leave and went to study in the Soviet Union, known today as

<u>Did you know?</u>

Mahmoud Darwish published more than 30 books of poetry and eight books of prose (writing that isn't poems). Today, even many years after his death, he's still considered the best Palestinian poet to have lived and is regarded as the national poet of Palestine.

Russia. He then moved to Egypt and Lebanon where he continued to live in exile until 1996 when he settled back in the West Bank.

Despite all the challenges he faced, Mahmoud Darwish continued to write throughout his life.

Edward Said

1935–2003

It was a brisk fall day in Jerusalem when Edward Said was born. The year was 1935 and Palestine was under the British Mandate, or British control. He had one younger sister and they grew up together in Jerusalem until his family moved to Cairo when Edward was 12 years old.

Edward felt that his school in Cairo was using colonial oppression and refused to listen to their rules, so one day, the school decided to kick him out. But this did not break his spirit. Instead, he went to another school, this time in the United States of America. He had a difficult time at first but he worked hard and ended up as the top student in the school!

Edward went on to study at Princeton University and then Harvard University. He was then appointed a professor at Columbia University. Because he was

Did you know?

While living in Cairo, Edward went to a school called Victoria College. There he was told, along with all the other children, that they were not allowed to speak their native languages—be it Arabic, Greek or Armenian— they could only speak English.

Did you know?

Said wrote many non-fiction books on subjects including Palestine, literature and culture. His most famous work is a book called *Orientalism*.

a hard worker who thought a lot about things, many people wanted to know his opinion and he was invited to teach and speak in many places.

Edward Said worked hard, but he also loved to enjoy life and he played the piano very well. He even opened an academy with his friend Daniel Barenboim in Berlin that, to this day, teaches music to students.

Samiha Khalil

1923–1999

Samiha was born in 1923 and attended school at a time when not all girls were able to do so. At the age of 17, however, she dropped out of high school to get married, and went on to have five children.

But this did not stop her from working hard to improve life for Palestinians, and women in particular.

Samiha eventually earned her high school degree 25 years after she got married, because it is never too late to achieve your goals! But even before she earned this diploma, Samiha did a lot to advance Palestinian society. Her contributions can still be seen today, even decades after her death.

One of her biggest contributions was founding Inash Alusra Association, the largest Palestinian welfare organization, which helps any Palestinian in need. It supports families in need and houses orphans, it provides developmental education for women and academic scholarships for students, and it tries to preserve Palestinian culture and heritage.

Fun Fact

Samiha started her charity work after the Nakba in 1948 (p 98). She used to collect money, clothes and food from those around her and give them to the needy.

Sometimes people disagreed with Samiha's beliefs. She would stage protests and was often sent to jail or put under house arrest. Still, she persisted in speaking up for what she believed in.

Samih al-Qasim

1939–2014

Samih al-Qasim was a Palestinian poet from a small town in the Galilee called Rameh. He was born in Zarqa, in present-day Jordan, because his father was serving in the army of King Abdullah at the time. The family soon went back to their little town where Samih attended school.

In many of his poems and writing, Samih talks about how he was a little boy—just nine years old—when the Nakba (p 98) happened.

Samih was lucky, in a way, because his village wasn't destroyed, and he and his family did not flee. Instead, Rameh came under Israeli rule and Samih and his family became Israeli citizens. Samih stayed true to his beliefs and was sent to jail several times because of this. Despite this, Samih continued to

Did you know?

Samih considers the Nakba to be his real birthday because his oldest memories are from that time.

teach and write about his beliefs and hopes.

Along with Mahmoud Darwish he is considered one of the most prominent poets of Palestine.

Did you know?

Samih wrote his first book at the age of 19 and over his career published more than 70 books including poems, prose and plays. He also worked as a journalist and an editor and publisher.

Mustafa Murrar

1929–2021

The writer Mustafa Murrar was born to a family of farmers in the Palestinian village of Jaljulia.

Fun Fact

Mustafa's village was so small it didn't even have a school. But Mustafa wanted to learn how to read and write, so he would walk to the neighboring city of Qalqilya to attend school.

Mustafa spent only seven years in school, but he was an avid reader who devoured anything that fell into his hands. That's why, in 1951, he was able to pass an exam that allowed him to attend a teaching school in Yaffa. By the time he finished his certification, Jaljulia had an elementary school and he became a teacher there. While teaching, he went on to get a degree and became the principal of the school, which he helped to grow and improve over the years.

Mustafa did all this even though he was an amputee with only one leg. You see, during the 1948 Arab–Israeli War, Mustafa was still a teenager. One night, while guarding his village along with some friends, bombs went off nearby. Mustafa did not die, but he lost his leg and for the rest of his life used a prosthetic limb.

Mustafa worked for over 30 years as a school principal and his love for reading and teaching was only surpassed by his love for writing. He wrote newspaper articles as well as novels, essays and short stories. His biggest love of all, however, was writing for children. So in 1982 he retired early to dedicate his life to writing.

Did you know?

By the time Mustafa Murrar died at 92 years old, he had published hundreds of stories and 86 books. Many of these were for children, which is why he has been called "the pillar of Palestinian children's literature."

Sahar Khalifeh

b. 1941

After Mahmoud Darwish, Sahar Khalifeh is the most translated Palestinian writer. But Sahar's rise to stardom was not easy.

Sahar was born in Nablus to a family of eight girls. Early on, she realized that life for a woman would not always be easy. When she finished high school, her family told her she had to get married, and she did, but she was very unhappy. It was not until over a decade later that she was able to leave her marriage. That was also when she decided to go to university. At 32 years old, she enrolled her two daughters in school and started at Birzeit University herself. She did very well and continued her education, eventually getting an MA and even a PhD from the United States.

Sahar describes in her memoir how the writing life was not always easy and how Ismail Shammout (p 52) encouraged her to keep going when she first started out.

Did you know?

Sahar Khalifeh is one of the most prolific female Palestinian writers of recent times. She has written 11 novels, which have been translated into many languages including English, French, German and Spanish.

For Sahar, Palestine would always be home, and she eventually returned following her studies. From there she wrote more novels and even opened up The Women and Family Affairs Center in Nablus to promote women's rights and gender equality within Palestinian society. She later opened more branches across the country. Many consider her the first feminist Palestinian writer.

صورة وأيقونة وعهد قديم
مذكرات إمرأة غير واقعية
لم نعد جواري لكم!
المتبار
عباد الشمس
حتى الأول

Malak Mattar

b. 2000

Malak lived most of her childhood during war. She often felt sad and afraid. One day, when she was 14, she took a piece of paper and started to sketch. She put everything she was feeling into that work, taking all the fears out of herself and channeling them into her first painting.

For 51 days, no one in the neighborhood went outside because of the war, and Malak continued to paint. This not only gave her something to do, but helped her to feel better because she was able to express what she was feeling through her art. Malak then decided to share her paintings on social media.

Although Malak was born in Gaza, her family are refugees from other parts of Palestine. Her life in Gaza and the stories she has heard from parents and grandparents have shaped the art she creates. Malak's paintings are beautiful and colorful, but

Did you know?

When people saw Malak's work, they loved it and started to share it widely. Malak would receive messages from people across the globe asking to buy her paintings. Malak continued to paint, and she has displayed her paintings in more than 60 exhibitions across the world!

sometimes they also tell sad stories. Her paintings show us how we can find beauty in any situation, and how expressing ourselves creatively can not only make us feel better, but can help

the whole world to understand our perspective.

Today, Malak is studying at university in Turkey, and she hopes to continue her studies in the United States, where she can keep painting and have many more exhibitions.

Ismail Shammout

1930–2006

On a hot day in July, when Ismail was 18 years old, his whole world turned upside down. He was at home with his parents and brothers and sisters, when soldiers came and told them they had to leave. The family of nine, along with everyone else in their village, started a long journey that day (*Nakba* p 98). They met nice people along the way who gave them food and shelter. In the end, Ismail's family found their way to Gaza where they lived in a refugee camp.

Ismail loved to paint and was soon hired as an art teacher. He continued to save money until he had $30, which back then was enough to get him to Cairo, in Egypt. There he went to art school, and in less than five years, he had created more than 60 oil paintings, watercolors and drawings.

Then one day, he packed them all up and went back to Gaza where he set up the first ever Palestinian art exhibition. The exhibition was so successful that he held more and more of them,

Did you know?

Ismail and his father and brothers made money by selling homemade halaweh desserts on the streets.

murals—wall paintings—called *Palestine: The Exodus and the Odyssey.*

Did you know?

Ismail continued to paint throughout his life. His paintings feature Palestinians and Palestinian symbolism. They show us, with color and paint, the experience of being Palestinian for the last 70 years. Many of his pieces are famous across the world.

and eventually attended art school in Italy.

One of his most famous projects was a collaboration with his wife, Tamam Alakhal. It is a series of 19 large

Shireen Abu Akleh
1971–2022

When Shireen Abu Akleh went to university, she realized she loved being close to people, sharing their stories and helping the world learn more about the struggles of Palestinians. Shireen studied journalism, then worked as a journalist and a field correspondent—that's someone who goes out to where things are happening to report on them—for Al Jazeera, one of the largest Arab news networks in the world.

Families across Palestine, and the Arab world, felt like they knew Shireen personally because she was always on TV reporting on what was happening in Palestine. Shireen was very brave, often going to places where there was war and conflict. She was scared when she went, but she overcame that fear because she had chosen journalism to be close to the people, and even if she couldn't change the reality of what was happening to the people, she could at least deliver their stories to the world.

> ### Did you know?
>
> When Shireen was a little girl, growing up in Beit Hanina (a suburb of Jerusalem), she thought she wanted to be an architect so she could build things that would last forever.

Shireen did build something that would last forever. She documented decades of personal stories and histories that will never be forgotten, because younger Palestinian generations will always be able to read and hear her words.

One day, while reporting from a Jenin refugee camp, Shireen was shot by the Israeli military. The entire world mourned her death, with thousands of people across Palestine and the world coming out to attend her funeral and honor her memory.

Agriculture

Historically, many Palestinians worked as farmers, so we're intimately familiar with the land and the beautiful things it can give us if we treat it well. We have countless wild plants that grow in the beautiful hills and mountains across the country, and Palestinians have found uses for almost all of these plants—from delicious foods to healthy teas. Some of the oldest agriculture methods in the world can be traced back to our part of the world. Many of these methods, like irrigated terraces, and plants like za'atar and olives, have become important cultural symbols for us too.

Olives & oil

Olive trees are very important to Palestinians. Throughout history, we've relied on olives and olive oil for our food, but also for our livelihood, since we sell them.

Did you know?

Palestinians love olive trees because they are very strong trees; they can grow in harsh conditions with very little water, and they have very tough, deep roots. So we think of ourselves like these olive trees; tough people in the face of any hardship.

Some of the oldest olive trees in the world are thought to be in Palestine and go back thousands of years. Their trunks become very wide; some can grow up to 30 feet or 10 meters in girth—that means it would take you at least 10 wide steps just to walk around the tree!

Fun Fact

Olive trees produce a lot of fruit every other year. They can bear olives in the off years, but the yield is so small it's only sufficient for the farming family and not for selling.

Palestinian families love to get together during the harvest season every year and pick their groves, often cooking under the trees and singing songs about the harvest. Many Palestinians will tell you that the best meal in the world is a piece of bread dipped in freshly pressed olive oil. It's so delicious!

The olives are picked between fall and winter—depending on whether you want green or black olives. Some of the olives are preserved or pickled for eating and the rest are pressed to make olive oil. Palestinians don't let anything go to waste—the old oil is used to make soap, and the leftover seeds from making oil are dried and used as wood for burning.

Za'atar

Za'atar is a wild herb that grows in the mountains of Palestine, Jordan, Syria and Lebanon. Palestinians have been foraging it for hundreds of years. Foraging means picking plants out in the wild. Many families love springtime because it's a chance to go out into the hills and mountains and pick the delicious plants that grow there.

Palestinians use it to make fresh salads or akras za'atar; a flat bread layered with za'atar, green onions and plenty of olive oil. The rest of the leaves are left to dry and they are then used in teas, in breads and of course for za'atar, the most famous Palestinian condiment of all.

Almost every Palestinian family has a small bowl of za'atar next to one of olive oil on its

Did you know?

There's nothing that quite compares to the beautiful smell and taste of the za'atar you pick by hand in the Palestinian mountains in the spring.

Fun Fact

When za'atar is first picked, its leaves are soft with a floral and peppery smell.

kitchen table, that kids and grown-ups alike dip bread in for breakfast, snacks or light suppers. The za'atar herb mix is made with dried za'atar leaves that are crushed super-fine and mixed with sesame seeds, salt and sumac, a sour spice made from berries that grow wild in Palestine. Palestinians love and live very closely with nature.

Za'atar is such a big part of our food, and it is also a cultural symbol (p 25).

Battir Terraces

Battir is a beautiful Palestinian village situated on hills outside Jerusalem that descend into a valley where the famous train track connects Jerusalem to Yaffa.

It is famous for an ancient irrigation system that was formed by people layering stones on the hill to create terraces. These terraces basically turned the mountain into large stairs, each held up by a wall, so that when water was transported down these steps—from springs or reservoirs using canals or sluices—it stayed in the fields and made cultivation easier. It really is a sight to behold. If you look at it from a distance, it appears like grassy stairs growing in the hills.

Vegetables and olives have been cultivated since then, and still are today. One of the most famous vegetables in Palestine is an eggplant known as "Battir eggplant" which has a very short season in the summer. The eggplant are a light purple hue and quite narrow and long. People love them and wait for them from year to year because they are so creamy and sweet.

While eggplant may be the crop Battir is best known for, so much more grows in this lush land; from olives and grapes to figs, apples and peaches. In fact, people colloquially refer to the village as "God's heaven on Earth" or "the basket of fruit and vegetables."

Did you know?

Throughout history, this ancient town had a good water supply and a brilliant irrigation system, which made it a center for agriculture. This irrigation system is still in use today and it is fed by seven springs that have been providing fresh water for about 2000 years!

Watermelon

Watermelons are a delicious fruit, especially in summer. They are sweet, crunchy and very juicy.

Palestinians love to eat watermelon, and they often serve it with salty white cheese because the contrast makes you want to come back for more and more. Palestinian watermelons, which were grown across the country from Jenin and the Jordan Valley all the way to Gaza, were famous across the Arab world for their sweetness and special taste. Although some watermelons are grown in greenhouses today, everyone says the traditional ones grown in the field have the best and most special taste!

But watermelons are more than just food for Palestinians—they carry a special significance and meaning. Can you guess why? The watermelon, like the Palestinian flag (p 26), is red, green, white and black! So it has become a symbol of Palestine for many people within the country and across the world.

There are many kinds of watermelon nowadays, from baby ones to elongated ones, from seedless red to bright yellow. But many believe the most delicious is the traditional kind with black seeds inside. Palestinians love the seeds of the watermelon, too. Roasted and salted watermelon seeds are one of the most popular snacks among Palestinians. It is common to find people sitting outside on breezy evenings, chatting with their friends while cracking seeds.

Native plants

Palestinians love to forage. Every season there are different things to forage for and it is always exciting to go out into the mountains and see what you can find.

Did you know?

You might be surprised to learn that some plants are edible and delicious because at first glance they look scary —like akoub!

Akoub is a thistle—a plant with thorns—that has many sharp spikes. Palestinians collect it and remove the spikes to reveal beautiful flower-like buds which are either fried or cooked in a stew.

Loof—known as Palestinian arum lily—is a poisonous plant that Palestinians eat. Don't worry though! We have learned over the years how to cook it so that it isn't harmful when eaten.

One of its most popular uses is in a dish called *ja'ajouleh*, a sort of dumpling soup.

Khubeizeh is another pretty plant—a mallow with green flower-shaped leaves—which is collected in late winter and early spring. The leaves are cooked down, usually with tiny pearls of dough, almost like baby pasta, and flavored with lots of crispy onions.

The mountains and hills of Palestine are filled with countless other herbs and plants like *meramiyeh*, a sage we put in tea, and many leaves, which are often stuffed with rice and meat. Those leaves often have very interesting names based on how they look: *elsayneh* or *Isan el thor* means "ox tongue" or "tongue leaves" because the leaves have a rough texture, while *za'amatot* or *qarn el ghazal* means "deer's antler" because the flowers of the plant look like antlers!

Cuisine

Did you know that even in a tiny country, food changes as you go from town to town? It all depends on what ingredients you have, what your traditions are and what you've been exposed to in the past. There are some dishes that everyone in the country knows and they're practically cultural symbols.

Palestinians share many of our dishes—like hummus, falafel and tabouleh—with our neighbors in Syria, Lebanon and Jordan because long ago, we didn't really have borders between us. We visited each other and ate together and learned from one another, the way neighbors do. But there are other dishes which are really special and unique to Palestinians. And do you know what all these dishes have in common? They're absolutely delicious!

Maqlubeh, Msakhan & Maftool

Maqlubeh is one of the most recognized Palestinian dishes.

There are many ways to make it and each family has their own recipe, but it's generally layers of rice and meat and fried vegetables. Some families include eggplant, some use cauliflower and others might choose carrot or a mix of all three.

Do you know what *maqlubeh* means? Flipped upside-down! It suits the dish perfectly because when cooking is done, you flip the pot upside down to reveal a cake-shaped dish of rice.

Msakhan is another famous Palestinian dish made around the olive harvest because it uses a lot of olive oil. In fact, all its ingredients are ones that Palestinian farmers grow themselves: from the onions and sumac to the olive oil and chicken. You have big pieces of *taboon* bread (a flat bread baked on stones in a special oven called a *taboon*), topped with onions that have been cooked down in olive oil until sweet, then mixed with sumac. Everything is broiled and topped with roast chicken. *Msakhan* means "reheated" and apparently, we call it this because the dish started out

as a way for farmers to reheat old *taboon* bread and make it taste better!

And finally, *Maftool* means "rolled." It's clear that we like to name many of our dishes to reflect the way they are made or cooked. *Maftool* are tiny pearls made from rolling wholewheat flour around grains of bulgur. These pearls are then steamed and served with a brothy stew, with sides such as chickpeas and chicken and sometimes butternut squash or tomato.

Did you know?

Legend has it that when Salah el-Din freed Jerusalem from the Crusaders over 800 years ago, Palestinians made him maqlubeh, which used to be called bathinjaniyeh (this means "eggplant dish"), to celebrate. He asked, "What is the name of this flipped upside-down dish?" and since then, people started to call it maqlubeh.

Mansaf & Mahashi

Cuisine in Palestine is more regional than national. This means that people from different regions of Palestine will eat different dishes. Of course, our foods are still very similar, but there are some interesting variations throughout the country, especially when we look at meals made specifically for an occasion or celebration.

Mansaf is one of the most recognized celebratory meals for Palestinians. It's a traditionally Bedouin (Bedouins are nomadic Arabs) dish made from dried yogurt that looks a lot like white tennis balls. Pieces of lamb are cooked in this yogurt sauce and then they are placed on top of a giant platter that is layered with *shrak* (a super thin bread) and rice, then drizzled with more of the yogurt sauce.

Another dish you will often find at happy occasions is *mahashi*. *Mahashi* simply means "stuffed things." It covers a whole range of vegetables that are stuffed with a rice mixture. The most popular vegetables used for stuffing are *koosa* (zucchini), eggplant and grape leaves, and the most common stuffing is rice and lamb. Sometimes the vegetables are cooked in tomato sauce and other times they are

Did you know?

As with *maqlubeh*, there are as many versions of mahashi as there are families in Palestine! But this is one dish that is as common on a weekly dining table in a Palestinian home as it is on a festive one.

served as a broth. There are also vegetarian versions that include rice but have herbs and other vegetables, like tomatoes and onions, instead of meat.

Knafeh

Knafeh is an ancient dessert made of crumbly or thin strands of dough that are stuffed with either crunchy nuts or stretchy cheese and then baked and soaked in sugar syrup. It is the most delicious sweet; every bite has you coming back for another!

Knafeh is usually made in large trays and sold at sweet shops, some of which have been around for hundreds of years. There are different kinds of *knafeh*. One of the most famous is *knafeh nabulsiyeh*, which simply means *knafeh* from Nablus, the place where it was first created.

Knafeh nabulsiyeh became so popular across the Arab world, that most *knafeh* is now made with cheese.

Nablus is so famous for this Palestinian dessert that in 2009 the city entered the Guinness Book of Records for the largest knafeh in the world. The plate weighed 3891 lbs/1765 kg and was 246 feet/ 75 meters long. That's as heavy as a rhinoceros and as long as a Boeing 747 airplane!

Ka'ak Al Quds

Ka'ak al Quds is a kind of bread that's shaped like a very long zero. It has a wonderfully crunchy crust with sesame seeds, and a soft, fluffy interior.

There are many bakeries that make this bread, but the oldest ones are found inside the walls of Jerusalem's Old City. The families who own these bakeries have been making this bread for

generations. The dough is made and left to rise overnight. Very early in the morning, the baker shapes it into a ring then dips it in a water and sesame mixture and keeps rolling it until it forms a ring that's about a foot and a half long. Once the breads are baked in wood-fired ovens, they are ready to go.

Fun Fact

Sellers pick up these breads in wooden trays. Some balance the trays on their heads, while others, who have bigger trays, put them on a two- or three-wheeled cart that they push with both hands. No matter what they choose, everyone sells it the same way; calling "kaaaaaaa'aaaaaaak… kaaaaaaa'aaaaaak" as they walk the streets of Jerusalem.

School children and workers gather around the sellers to pick up their meal for the day. Along with each *ka'ak*, you get some *za'atar* wrapped in newspaper scraps, and if you want to really splurge, then you can also buy a very large falafel, or eggs that have been roasted in hay. You then rip a piece of *ka'ak*, crack and peel your egg, and you dip it all in *za'atar* as you enjoy bites from your meal. If you visit Jerusalem, this is the one dish you don't want to miss!

كعك

Hummus & Falafel

Hummus and falafel are the shared street foods of the countries in the Levant (Syria, Lebanon, Palestine and Jordan). Each country prepares and serves the dishes in a slightly different way, but you would have a hard time finding someone from any of these countries who did not grow up enjoying these staple dishes.

Falafel is made of chickpeas, but the chickpeas are not cooked, they are just soaked in water and then ground with herbs and spices and shaped into balls before frying. You can't help munching them right away when you get them fresh from the

Did you know?

The word hummus means "chickpea" in Arabic and we use that same word to refer to the smooth dip we make when mixing chickpeas with tahini.

fryer of a vendor on the old city streets of Jerusalem!

In Palestine, hummus and falafel are a big part of the culture. Every neighborhood, village and city has its own hummus and falafel shop (or stand), where people

may go at the weekend to get breakfast, or on a weeknight to get dinner, or in the middle of the day for a quick and filling lunch. They are very affordable but also healthy.

Whichever way you choose to enjoy these iconic Palestinian dishes, one thing's for sure: you will be coming back for them time and time again.

Performing Arts

People have been performing for entertainment—dancing, singing, acting—since the start of civilization. This tradition is particularly rich in Arab cultures, where some of the oldest evidence of performances can be found from thousands of years ago. Palestine is home to several ancient traditions, like *dabke* (p 84) and *zajal* (p 86), but has also embraced newer arts like film and modern music. You can explore these wonderful performing arts over the next few pages and learn more about some of Palestine's best performers.

Palestinian Cinema

Palestine's movie industry is fairly young, but it has still made a big mark on the world.

Palestinian cinema has become so popular recently that in 2021, Netflix launched a *Palestinian Stories* collection, which features 32 films either about or created by Palestinians.

You know what makes these movies so special though? It's the people who create them and star in them; and there are many wonderful Palestinian movie directors and actors.

Hany Abu-Assad is one of those film directors. He has created many award-winning movies with *Paradise Now* even winning a Golden Globe. Hany says that the issues Palestinians deal with are what inspire much of his work.

While these directors work tirelessly behind the scenes, we get to know the actors on the screen. Some, like actress Hiam Abbass, star not only in Palestinian movies, but in mainstream movies and TV shows in the United States too. Other actors, like Saleh Bakri, come from a family of actors— his father and brothers are all also actors.

There are so many more movies, directors and actors that make Palestinian cinema special. And since it's a young industry, you can be sure you'll continue to discover more in the years to come.

Did you know?

Another brilliant director is Annemarie Jacir. In addition to her movies winning many awards, she also writes poems and stories, she teaches at universities and one year she organized the largest traveling film festival in Palestine.

Dabke

If you have ever been to a Palestinian wedding, then you have definitely seen a *dabke* performance!

There are many variations, or types, of *dabke*. The rhythm of the words sung for the dance, as well as the specific movements performed with the hands and legs, and also who is dancing or leading the troupes, changes in each and every version.

Sahjeh is a very famous Palestinian *dabke*, which involves clapping the hands together to a specific rhythm. *Dala'ona* is one of the most popular types of song to which people perform *dabke* today. It is usually a song with four verses of poetry where the first three lines have a rhyming or similar ending, while the last verse ends on a note that rhymes with *dala'ona*.

One of the most beautiful things about *dabke* is that it is performed in groups and everyone is coordinated so you really feel like you are part of a connected community. Also, the songs are usually very meaningful, and the words tell stories, so you are able to really express yourself and share in the occasion for which you are dancing.

Zajal

Music is such a big part of Palestinian culture, but music is not just singing or playing an instrument. There are many different kinds of poetry and styles of singing in Arabic music.

One of the most famous types is called *zajal*. It is semi-improvised which means the person performing it is often making up the words as they go along, but with a specific pattern, and its delivery is somewhere between speaking and singing. *Zajal* is fun because it is usually performed as a debate between *zajjalin* (poets who improvise the *zajal*).

The words can be funny, sad or happy, but they always make you feel something.

Did you know?

Zajal is often accompanied by percussive musical instruments like a derbake and daf—the derbake is a goblet drum and the daf a tambourine-like instrument—and sometimes even wind instruments like a shebabeh—a sort of flute.

Zajal has many different forms, and each relies on certain rhythms, lyrics and syllables. *Maijana, Ataaba, Rozana* and *Abu Alzuluf* are all different

Unfortunately, many of these traditions are starting to disappear, so it's so important that children learn about and remember these fun traditions so we can keep them alive for generations to come.

kinds of *zajal*. *Zaghareet* (singular: *zaghroota*) are a form of *zajal*—they are verses often spoken by women during special occasions, like weddings, at the end of which all the women respond with an ululation that sounds like *lulululeeeeeeesh*.

Fun Fact

If you have ever been to a Palestinian wedding, you have definitely heard a zaghroota or two!

Mohammed Assaf
b. 1989

Mohammed Assaf has been singing since he was a little boy living in Gaza. He started out singing at weddings and local events even though he never formally learned how to sing—he just had a natural talent for it.

When he was in his early twenties, he decided to try out for a singing show in the Middle East called *Arab Idol*. But to get to the show, Mohammed had to leave Gaza, which is not always an easy thing to do. He spent two days stuck at the border between Gaza and Egypt, trying to convince the border guards to let him through. When he finally got in and made it to the show's audition, the doors were closed. He had missed his chance.

But Mohammed did not give up— he jumped over a wall and got into the hotel where the show auditions were taking place. Still, he was too late and they would not give him a number. So what did Mohammed do? He started singing!

Did you know?

When people heard Mohammed sing, they were so amazed that one contestant gave up his own number so Mohammed could enter the contest. Mohammed became the most popular contestant to ever join *Arab Idol*.

The entire Arab world cheered for the little Palestinian boy who defied all odds to make it to the stage.

Mohammed won the contest by a landslide and has been singing professionally since. Many consider him the most famous Palestinian singer in the world.

Simon Shaheen

b. 1955

Simon Shaheen was born in the lush mountain village of Tarshiha in the Galilee in 1955. Even though his family moved to Haifa when he was two years old, he continued to spend much of his time—like weekends and holidays—in his original hometown where he and his family were surrounded by music.

You see, Simon's father, Hikmat, was a music teacher and *oud* player. Simon's brother, Najib, makes *ouds* himself and his sisters Laura and Rosette are also singers.

Simon has been playing the oud since he was five years old. He studied music his whole life and left Palestine to go to the United States and continue his education. Simon performs music at many famous events in order to preserve and share our musical traditions while allowing new people to appreciate them.

Did you know?

The oud is one of the most widely used instruments in Arabic music. It is a string instrument, like a guitar, but it is shaped differently with a short neck and a pear-shaped body, making the sound that comes out of it unique.

He also leads the Arabic music ensemble *Qantara* as well as the Arabic Music Retreat, a group that teaches Arabic music to students in the US.

Today Simon continues to play his music around the world, and he also participates in cross-cultural projects. This means projects that bring together

Fun Fact

Simon was so good at music that he created the Near Eastern Music Ensemble, a group of musicians from around the Arab world.

music traditions from around the world to show how rich our music, and lives, can be when we learn from one another.

Dalal Abu Amneh

b. 1983

Singer Dalal Abu Amneh was born in the city of Nazareth to a family who all love to sing and play music.

> ### Fun Fact
>
> Dalal is recognized for her very strong voice, which she says she inherited from her mother and her grandfather.

Dalal grew up in a big family and was always a hard worker. In fact, while Dalal is most recognized as a singer across the Arab world, she is also a doctor of neuroscience, studying how the brain functions. She was inspired to pursue this career because two of her sisters are hearing-impaired and she wanted to make a contribution towards improving their lives and the lives of others who have this disability.

Dalal is also passionate about preserving Palestinian culture and sharing it with others and she uses her music to achieve this. By the time she was 16, many people in the music world had taken notice of her strong voice. Dalal has sung in orchestras and festivals across the world and her songs are always performed in the Palestinian Arabic dialect.

Dalal also highlights the role elderly women have in preserving folklore and often features them in her musical projects. While she produces her own songs, she has also revived many of the traditional Palestinian folk songs from previous generations and successfully found a way to modernize them so that young people can enjoy these beautiful traditions.

Fun Fact

Dalal started singing when she was just four years old.

SANCTAE CATHARINAE VIRGINI ET MARTIRI DI CATVM

History & Religion

Palestine is a small country that has played a huge role in history! It is one of the oldest inhabited places on Earth, where people have lived, prospered and fought over the rich and valuable land. Jerusalem (p 10), its capital, is the heart of the world's three major monotheistic religions—Judaism, Christianity and Islam. Monotheistic means believing in only one God. Here, we'll discover Palestine's religious significance, how it is intertwined in its history and the events that have unfolded recently.

Ancient History

This land is treasured because of where it's located. It connects Egypt to Syria, and through it pass the main roads from the Mediterranean to the hills beyond the Jordan River.

The last empire to rule this land was the Ottoman Empire, but that empire fell apart after World War I and England began to control and administer Palestine. During that time, there was a plan to make Palestine a national homeland for Jewish people, who were facing persecution and believed this to be their promised land. As a result of the 1948 war, many Palestinians lost their land and homes and became refugees and the state of Israel was established. Today, Palestinians continue to advocate for an independent and free state to allow those who were expelled to return.

But it's not just the geographic location that made this land so significant and unique; it was also its importance to the world's three primary monotheistic religions. Those three religions are Judaism, Christianity and Islam. These three religions don't always exist peacefully together, but they actually have a lot in common, worshipping the same God and following similar principles that stem from the same past.

In fact, all three religions are called Abrahamic religions because they trace their history back to Abraham. People believe that 4000 years ago, Abraham decided to follow one God and left his home to travel across the present-day Middle East. Jews believe they are descendants of Abraham's son Isaac, while Muslims believe they are descendants of Abraham's son Ishmael.

Al Nakba

Palestinians use the word *nakba* to refer to a period in our history when we faced a time of catastrophe. We commemorate and remember this time every year on the 15th of May, although many Palestinians will tell you we remember it every single day.

Between 1947 and 1949 there was a war going on in the land of Palestine. An international body called the United Nations wanted to divide the land between the Jews and Palestinians, but the Palestinian population and surrounding Arab countries did not consider the division of their

land to be fair. Following the war, the state of Israel was established. In the process, almost 750,000 Palestinians, or half of our population at the time, lost their homes, were displaced, became refugees and had to leave Palestine. Some went to other countries; some stayed but had to go to refugee camps in other areas. It is this loss that our people refer to as *Al Nakba*.

But Palestinians are a strong people and many of those who left have built good lives, become successful and contributed to the societies they live in, as you've seen. But we never forget our homeland. To this day, Palestinians dream of being able to return and to live peacefully with everyone, and continue to work hard to make it a reality.

The key symbolizes this very dream. When Palestinians left Palestine during the *Nakba*, many locked their houses and took their keys with them because they thought they would return very soon. Even though it has been over 75 years since then, everyone who left has kept their key, to symbolize their hope of returning home one day.

Al Naksa

After the *Nakba*, life changed in Palestine for many people. Around three quarters of the country was now administered by the newly-founded State of Israel, while the remaining parts were administered by Jordan and Egypt.

For almost twenty years after 1948, fighting continued. Then in 1967, war erupted between Israel and its surrounding Arab countries—Syria, Jordan and Egypt. This war lasted for six days and the result of the conflict meant Israel now had control over the whole of Palestine including Gaza, the West Bank and East Jerusalem, and even territories from the other countries too, like the Sinai Peninsula and the Golan Heights.

The word *naksa* means "setback" and Palestinians use it to describe this war because, rather than help them reclaim their land, the Six-Day War set them back further with a loss of more territory.

While it may be sad to read about a history that is filled with wars, Palestinians have shown the world that they are a resilient and proud people. Even in the face of many of these adversities,

Did you know?

Palestinians commemorate this day every year on the 5th of June.

Palestinians continue to have hope that the future will be better and advocate for this hopeful vision in many ways. One of the ways we work for this better future is by preserving Palestinian culture for future generations and sharing it with others, so that they may learn more about our story, our beautiful and incredibly rich traditions and our history.

Islam

Islam is a monotheistic religion and Muslims believe in one God, whom they call Allah. They also believe that the prophet Muhammad is Allah's messenger and that Allah is all merciful, all powerful and unique. The Quran is the primary scripture, or book, of Islam. It is believed that the Quran is the word of God, revealed to His prophet Muhammad. Along with the Quran, the teachings and practices (called the *Sunnah*), and the traditional accounts (called *Hadith*) of Muhammad help to guide the followers of Islam.

Jerusalem is a very special place for Muslims because it is home to Al-Aqsa Mosque, one of the three holiest sites in Islam. The other two sites are located in Makkah, the house of God called the *Kaaba*, and in Medina, where the prophet is buried at Al-Masjid al-Nabawi, in Saudi Arabia.

Did you know?

Islam is the second largest religion in the world. About one quarter of the world today is Muslim. In the Arab world, however, Islam is the main religion and about 90% of the Arab population is Muslim.

Islam follows a lunar calendar—a calendar based on the moon. Its holy days fall on the same day of the lunar calendar every year, but that means they come at different times using Gregorian calendars.

In Palestine, these holidays are special and a time for families to get together, eat, celebrate and wish each other well. Children buy new clothes and visit relatives where they are often given money in place of gifts. Of course, food is a big part of these holidays too. For *Eid al Fitr*, *ka'ak* and *ma'amoul*—semolina cookies stuffed with dates or nuts—are found in every home. For *Eid al Adha* it's meat that takes center stage as families sacrifice animals, usually lamb, to feed the needy and themselves the most delicious meals.

Did you know?

The two major holidays or festivals are *Eid al Fitr* which comes after Ramadan, the month of fasting, and *Eid al Adha* which coincides with the Hajj pilgrimage.

Christianity

Christianity originated in the Middle East—in Palestine, to be exact!

Christianity is a monotheistic religion based on the life and teachings of Jesus of Nazareth. Jesus was born in Bethlehem (p 22) but grew up in Nazareth (p 18), the town his parents Mary and Joseph were from. Christians believe that Jesus is the Son of God, and that he was sent to Earth to bring salvation to its people. The main book of Christianity is the Bible and it is split into two parts—the Old Testament and the New Testament. Together, they teach its followers how to do good in the world, how to treat each other and how to be moral people.

Today there are different branches of Christianity, and while they might celebrate some holidays on different days and follow slightly different rules or traditions, they all adhere to the same primary teachings of Christianity.

The main holidays Christians in Palestine celebrate are Christmas and Easter. One of the most incredible and exciting moments of Christmas in Palestine is the Mass, or prayer, held on Christmas Eve in the Church of the Nativity in Bethlehem, where it is believed Jesus was born! Easter, also sometimes called *Eid al Kbeer* or "the big holiday," is celebrated across the country but is especially momentous in Jerusalem at the Church of the Holy Sepulchre where it is believed Jesus was crucified and resurrected. Both holidays are beautiful sights to behold and Christians from across the world flock to witness those holidays in the place where Christianity itself was born.

Index

Reem Kassis

Reem Kassis is a Palestinian writer and cookbook author. Although she studied business and psychology at UPenn and LSE, she chose a writing career in order to preserve the traditions and stories of Palestinians for her two daughters (soon to be three!) and to share them with the world. She has written two cookbooks and many chapters and articles, but this is the first children's book that she has written, and she hopes you will enjoy reading it as much as she loved writing it for you!

Noha Eilouti

Noha Eilouti is a Palestinian-Canadian illustrator and visual development artist, with a BSc in Multimedia Design from the American University of Sharjah, UAE. She is passionate about bringing stories to life through art. She enjoys traditional drawing, painting and traveling.

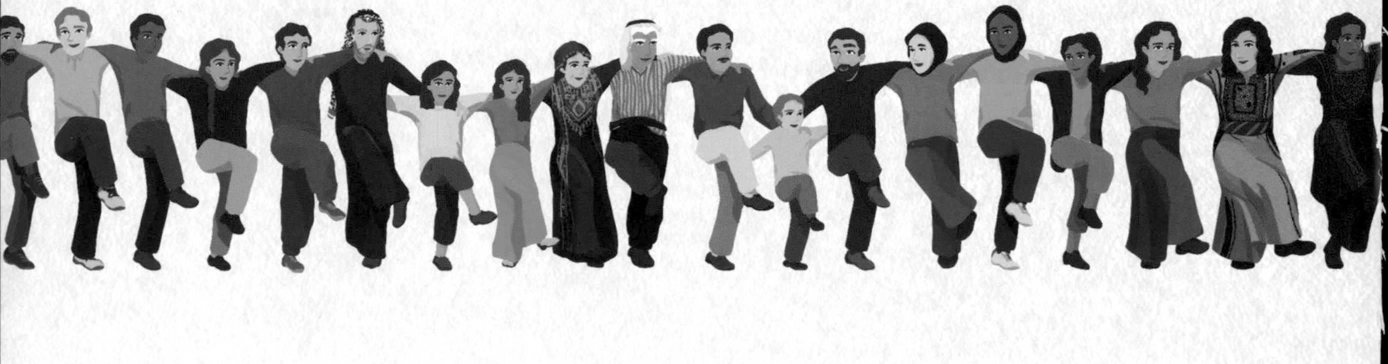